Columbia University

Contributions to Education

Teachers College Series

No. 181

AMS PRESS

NEW YORK

STATE RESPONSIBILITY FOR THE SUPPORT OF EDUCATION IN GEORGIA

BY

GORDON G. SINGLETON, Ph.D.

Teachers College, Columbia University
Contributions to Education, No. 181

Published by
Teachers College, Columbia University
New York City
1925

Library of Congress Cataloging in Publication Data

Singleton, Gordon Grady, 1890-
    State responsibility for the support of education in
Georgia.

    Reprint of the 1925 ed., issued in series: Teachers
College, Columbia University. Contributions to educa-
tion, no. 181.
    Originally presented as the author's thesis, Columbia.
    Bibliography: p.
    1. Education--Georgia--Finance. I. Title.
II. Series: Columbia University. Teachers College.
Contributions to education, no. 181.
LB2826.G4S5 1972   379.758   73-177779
ISBN 0-404-55181-5

Reprinted by Special Arrangement with Teachers
College Press, New York, New York

From the edition of 1925, New York
First AMS edition published in 1972
Manufactured in the United States

AMS PRESS, INC.
NEW YORK, N. Y.   10003

ACKNOWLEDGMENTS

The writer desires to acknowledge his indebtedness for and express his appreciation of the help he has received from students in the second major course in educational administration and from members of the faculty of Teachers College, and for the coöperation accorded him by the Georgia State Department of Education and other state departments.

Especially does he wish to acknowledge his indebtedness to Professors George D. Strayer, Fletcher Harper Swift, Edward S. Evenden, James R. McGaughy, Paul R. Mort, and Dr. Carter Alexander, of Teachers College, for their very valuable criticisms and suggestions.

He wishes also to express his gratitude to Professor Swift for a critical reading of each chapter during its preparation, and for the consequent invaluable suggestions, and to Professor Strayer for his interest, encouragement and guidance throughout the study.

Lastly, he acknowledges his great indebtedness to his wife for her inspiration and help.

TABLE OF CONTENTS

LIST OF TABLES

STATE RESPONSIBILITY FOR THE SUPPORT OF EDUCATION IN GEORGIA

CHAPTER I

INTRODUCTION

The purpose of this study is to determine the responsibility of the state for the support of education in Georgia and to propose a plan for its accomplishment.

That education is a function of the state has been assumed not only by the leaders of American educational thought and practice, but by our foremost statesmen. Evidence of the assumption of this principle by the state of Georgia from her earliest beginnings is to be found in at least three important sources or classes of sources: (1) State constitutions; (2) laws enacted by the General Assembly; (3) what, for the lack of a better term, may be called practical considerations. It will be well at the outset to consider briefly in turn the evidence furnished by each of these sources.

The constitutions of the state of Georgia have recognized education as a function of the state and have accordingly assumed the responsibility for the support of education in Georgia. When the colony of Georgia overthrew the control of England in 1776 and became an independent state, a convention of delegates meeting in Savannah drew up a constitution. "One of the most striking provisions of the constitution was the direction given to the legislature to establish free schools in each county to be supported at the general expense of the state."[1] The power and responsibility of the state for the support of education was recognized and set forth in the Constitution of 1798 and in all succeeding constitutions. Article VII, Section 1, Paragraph I, of the present constitution was adopted in 1877. It provides: "The powers of taxation over the whole state shall be exercised by the General Assembly for the following purposes only:

"For the support of the state government and the public institutions.
"For educational purposes."[2]

[1] R. P. Brooks, *History of Georgia*, p. 105.
[2] Georgia School Code, 1923, Section 1, p. 5.

The General Assembly, acting upon the principles enunciated in the state constitution, has regularly assumed the power and exercised the responsibility of the state for the support of the education by authorizing counties to levy taxes for the support of public schools within the county and by making annual appropriations for the support of education in Georgia.

Practical considerations clearly show the wisdom of our forefathers in accepting the principle that education is a function of the state and assuming responsibility for its support. They recognized the fact that there is no service rendered to all the people by the state so fundamental as that of education. That the welfare of the state demands this service since the welfare of a democratic state depends upon an enlightened and happy electorate. The representatives, officials, and laws of a state very generally reflect the electorate. A citizen living in one county this year may be living in another next year, and a child reared in a county which attaches little importance to education, and consequently makes little provision for education, may spend his adult life in a city in an extreme section of the state. Again, the price of a commodity manufactured in one section of the state for sale within the state, and hence the welfare of that industry, will depend upon the ability of the other sections to purchase it. The welfare of the whole state is then very decidedly dependent upon the welfare of the other counties which make up the state. Then, in the light of the above considerations, we may say that the state has rightly assumed the responsibility for the support of education.

Just how this responsibility may be most scientifically determined and fulfilled, and just what its implications are, is a problem which is receiving the most serious and intelligent consideration of the lay and educational leaders, not only in Georgia, but in all the states of the Union. The meaning of the problem, state responsibility for the support of education, has generally found expression in the phrases, "equalization of educational opportunity" and "equalization of school support." One of the best interpretations of these phrases is expressed in Volume I of the Educational Finance Inquiry, viz:

To carry into effect the principle of "equalization of educational opportunity" and "equalization of school support" as commonly understood it would be necessary (1) to establish schools or make other arrangements sufficient to furnish the children in every locality within the state with equal educational opportunities up to some prescribed minimum; (2) to raise the funds necessary for this purpose by local or state taxation adjusted in such manner as to bear upon the people in all localities at the same rate in relation to their tax-paying ability, and (3) to provide adequately either for the supervision and control of all the schools, or for their direct administration, by a state department of education.[3]

Even a cursory study of existing educational conditions in Georgia reveals glaring inequalities in both the educational offering and the support of education in proportion to tax-paying ability. These inequalities clearly indicate that the present system of school support is not accomplishing the purpose so laudably cherished by the makers of the constitution and the legislators who have annually voted appropriations for the support of education. That this is true is further evidenced by the fact that there is a general belief and desire upon the part of the legislators and people that something should be done to insure equality of opportunity of at least a minimum educational offering and to provide for equalization of school support.

The Problem: It is the purpose of the present study to determine the means and methods (1) whereby every child in the State of Georgia may be insured at least minimum offering, regardless of where he or she may live, and (2) whereby the cost will be distributed equally throughout the state in proportion to the ability of the component political units to pay.

The Sources and Method: It is scarcely necessary to state that the present study is based almost entirely upon original documents. Those which have been found most useful are: Documents issued by the State Department of Education, including the report of the survey made in 1923, and the Georgia School Code; Comptroller-General's annual reports and files; regular and special reports of the State Tax Commission; publications of the Census Bureau; bulletins of the United States

[3] G. D. Strayer and Robert M. Haig, *The Financing of Education in the State of New York*, p. 174.

Bureau of Education, together with certain other material found valuable. The method will be largely statistical and documentary.

Limitations: It seems advisable, in order that the reader may approach intelligently the data presented in the following chapters, to indicate at the outset certain handicaps which have been encountered: (1) In seeking a measure of comparative financial ability it has been necessary to depend upon assessed valuation, as no data and no means were found by which true valuation could be determined accurately. (2) It has long been recognized that enrollment is an unsatisfactory basis for arriving at a measure of the educational task or burden of a community, county, or state. Nevertheless, in the case of Georgia, in dealing with individual schools it has been necessary to employ enrollment rather than average daily attendance, because average daily attendance is reported to the State Department of Education for counties only. (3) Again, costs and other data are not reported separately for elementary schools and for high schools. The importance of making such a distinction can hardly be over-emphasized in view of the well-known fact that it costs from two to two and one-half times as much to educate a child in high school as in elementary school.[4] (4) Another obstacle which must be faced by one who wishes to study Georgia's system of school support is the fact that in reporting enrollment of individual schools, no distinction is made between white and colored children. This affects directly the computation of the number of pupils per teacher, cost per child, and other important factors.[5] (5) More significant than any of the handicaps thus far mentioned is the fact that the official reports do not separate expenditures for capital outlay from expenditures for current expenses. In like manner, costs for debt service are not reported separately. Moreover, the methods employed in reporting costs do not afford any means whereby the scientific student can work out these very essential distinctions.

[4] California gives definite recognition to this fact in the law which requires the county to give $30 per elementary school child and $60 per high school child. *See* F. H. Swift: *Studies in Public School Finance. The West.*

[5] See the *Annual Report* of the State Superintendent of Schools for 1923. This distinction is made for counties and for the state as a whole, but is of little service in a study dealing with individual schools.

In the immediately following chapters, the solution of our problem will be considered under the following divisions:

1. The measurement of educational need.
2. The determination of the minimum educational offering which the state should equalize and support.
3. An adequate measurement of the ability of each unit to support its schools.
4. A plan of school support based upon these findings.

CHAPTER II

A MEASURE OF EDUCATIONAL NEED IN GEORGIA

Any study which has as its purpose the development of a system of state fiscal support must first concern itself with the determination of a technique for the measurement of the educational needs of the various units of the state.

By educational need, as considered in this study, is meant the cost of providing the minimum educational offering set up by the state. The educational need then of any community will be the cost to that community of providing the minimum educational offering set up by the state. The measure of this need will be the cost expressed in terms of some common unit.[1]

With the exception of certain minor appropriations, Georgia now distributes all her state aid to the counties upon the basis of school census; in other words, the unit now employed in Georgia to measure educational need is the census child. This method, although one of the most commonly employed in the United States, is no longer defended by even those states which employ it. The cost to a community of providing education does not depend upon the number of children in the school census, but upon those who are in school.

Another defect in this method may be shown by a single example: In a thickly populated county the pupils may be grouped in large schools with 35 pupils or more per teacher, while in a thinly populated county the pupils are so scattered that there are many one-teacher schools with 25 pupils or less per teacher. It will require many more teachers to provide for the pupils in the latter county. In view of the fact that the teacher's salary constitutes 75 per cent or more of the total current expenses, it follows that the total cost of maintaining public schools will be much greater in the county employing the larger number of teachers, provided equally well qualified and consequently equally well paid teachers are employed.

[1] Paul R. Mort, *The Measurement of Educational Need*, Chaps. I and II.

In view of the facts just stated, it should be evident that one of the two factors which may be used in measuring educational need is the number of teachers to be employed, the other factor being the expenditure per teacher. The supreme significance of the teacher as a factor in school costs has already been recognized by a number of our states in their methods of apportioning state funds. New York State distributes 91 per cent of the state fund for education on a teacher basis.[2] North Carolina has adopted the teacher as a measure of need and a basis of distributing state aid.[3] Massachusetts apportions 83.4 per cent of the state funds for education on the per-teacher basis.[4] Again, although California raises both state and county moneys for elementary schools on a per-pupil basis, she apportions them on a per-teacher basis.[5] Further support for the practice of employing the teacher as the unit for measuring cost in the different divisions of the school system is found in the results obtained by the Educational Finance Inquiry Commission.[6] For these and other reasons, it was decided to employ current expenses per teacher as the unit of measurement of educational need in the present study.

The present chapter will concern itself with the problem of determining the number of teachers to be employed, reserving for Chapter III the consideration of the problem of expenditure per teacher.

The first question to be answered in determining the educational need of any community is: To how many teacher units is such a community entitled? If educational opportunities are to be equalized, each community of the state must be provided with as many teachers as the average number for the state. For example, if in a given state it is found that on the average one teacher is employed for every 35 children enrolled in school, the demands of equalization will require that this be the basis employed in estimating the number of teachers to which each and

---

[2] George D. Strayer and Robert M. Haig, *The Financing of Education in the State of New York*, p. 98.

[3] F. W. Morrison. Unpublished Ph.D. Thesis.

[4] F. H. Swift, *Studies in Public School Finance. The East*, p. 54, Table XIX.

[5] F. H. Swift, *Studies in Public School Finance. The West*, pp. 108–10.

[6] George D. Strayer and Robert M. Haig, *The Financing of Education in the State of New York*, p. 43, f.n.l.

every community is entitled. The measure here suggested, as will be shown, is too crude and inaccurate for a scientific study of educational need. In such a study, it is necessary, while applying this principle, to refine our measures through the grouping of communities on the basis of some common fundamental characteristic such as the type of school maintained, e. g., communities maintaining one-teacher schools, communities maintaining two-teacher schools, communities maintaining three-teacher schools, etc.

In view of the facts just stated, it will be necessary to determine the average number of pupils per teacher in communities maintaining a one-teacher school, a two-teacher school, a three-teacher school, etc. In making such computations, it would be desirable, if possible, to determine the number of pupils in average daily attendance per teacher, but, as explained in Chapter I, the state of Georgia does not report average daily attendance for individual schools. It is necessary therefore to accept and utilize the only data available for this purpose, namely, enrollment.

In order to determine the average number of pupils per teacher in communities of different types, the communities of Georgia were classified on the basis of the number of teachers employed, beginning with communities maintaining one-teacher schools and ending with those maintaining a nineteen-teacher school, thus giving, in all, nineteen classes of communities.

In order to find the number of pupils per teacher in one-teacher schools, Table I was compiled. This table shows the total number of one-teacher schools classified on the basis of enrollment, variations in enrollment in such schools, the number of schools corresponding to each enrollment given, the number of teachers, and finally, the number of pupils per teacher. It is evident that from such a table may readily be computed the average, the median, and the quartile enrollments per teacher, as well as the range of enrollment.

TABLE I

ENROLLMENT OF ONE-TEACHER SCHOOLS OF VARIOUS
SIZES IN 1923

Enrollment	Number of One-Teacher Schools	Number of Teachers	Total Enroll- ment	Per Teacher Enroll- ment
0 to 4	2	2	4	2
5 " 9	18	18	126	7
10 " 14	68	68	816	12
15 " 19	163	163	2,771	17
20 " 24	250	250	5,500	22
25 " 29	277	277	7,479	27
30 " 34	231	231	7,392	32
35 " 39	237	237	8,769	37
40 " 44	190	190	7,980	42
45 " 49	113	113	5,311	47
50 " 54	76	76	3,952	52
55 " 59	36	36	2,052	62
60 " 64	13	13	806	57
65 " 69	16	16	1,072	67
70 " 74	5	5	360	72
75 " 79	1	1	77	77
80 " 84	1	1	82	82
85 " 89				
90 " 94	1	1	92	92
120 " 124	1	1	122	122
Total	1,699	1,699	54,763	

Average Per-Teacher Enrollment -------------	32
Median " " " -------------	32
Q_1 " " " -------------	23
Q_3 " " " -------------	41
Range " " " -------------	2–122

From Table I we see that the average enrollment per teacher
in one-teacher schools varies all the way from 2 to 122 pupils.
The enrollment in the typical (median) school is 32. It will
be observed that one-fourth of the one-teacher schools have an
enrollment of 41 or more, and that another fourth of the one-
teacher schools have an enrollment of 23 or less. The average
enrollment per teacher (obtained by dividing the total enrollment by the total teachers) in all one-teacher schools in Georgia
was found to be 33.

The One-Teacher School. The variations in the average enrollment per teacher revealed by Table I (last column) and a

knowledge of the local conditions which lie back of these situations, and which necessitate the maintenance of large numbers of one-teacher schools regardless of small enrollment, make evident the impossibility of computing on the basis of average enrollment, median enrollment, or any other similar basis, the number of teachers to be allowed one-teacher schools. In other words, the one-teacher school constitutes a distinct problem, and in measuring educational need we shall be obliged to allow one teacher for every such school, regardless of enrollment. On the other hand, not more than one teacher will be allowed, lest when we come to the distribution of funds on a per-teacher basis, we encourage the continuance of one-teacher schools where two or more teachers should be employed. For it is easy to see that any policy which permitted a one-teacher school to receive grants for two or three teachers without actually employing more than one teacher would place a premium upon the perpetuation of a bad condition, to say nothing of the injustice to other communities similarly situated but making better provisions for their children. Again, computing the number of teachers to be allowed for one-teacher schools on the basis of a state average number of pupils per teacher would work a grave injustice to sparsely settled counties where the number of such schools with small enrollments is large.

The purpose of presenting Table I at this point was primarily to show the method employed in determining the average number of pupils per teacher. This same method was utilized in dealing with the problem for each of the nineteen classes of communities already defined.

The results obtained by applying this method to all schools in the state employing one teacher, to all schools employing two teachers, to all schools employing three teachers, etc., were tabulated, as shown in Table I, and the findings were consolidated into Table II.

TABLE II

PER-TEACHER ENROLLMENT IN SCHOOLS OF
VARIOUS SIZES

Number of Teachers in School	Average	Median	Q_1	Q_3	Range
1	32	32	23	41	2–122
2	31	31	25	37	9– 69
3	31	31	26	37	9– 66
4	32	32	26	37	19– 75
5	34	33	26	41	17– 66
6	32	33	28	38	19– 50
7	34	33	27	38	16– 67
8	33	33	27	40	19– 51
9	33	34	27	38	20– 60
10	31	31	27	33	21– 46
11	32	32	30	34	19– 41
12	33	32	27	37	16– 46
13	33	33	29	35	21– 38
14	32	31	27	37	20– 43
15	34	34	29	37	28– 50
16	34	33	29	34	26– 44
17	34	34	28	36	26– 44
18	33	33	28	37	21– 38
19	34	33	28	35	21– 38

Table II shows the average enrollment, the median enrollment, Q_1 and Q_3, and the range in the enrollment for all schools of different sizes, e.g., for one-teacher schools, for two-teacher schools, for three-teacher schools, etc. It is interesting to note the great variation that exists in the enrollment of different classes of communities. We get a more accurate idea of the variation when we see that in the two-teacher school, for instance, one-fourth have a per-teacher enrollment of 25 (Q_1) or less, while another one-fourth of the two-teacher schools have a per-teacher enrollment of 37 (Q_3) or more. The variation, however, is a little less in most of the types of communities.

What is of much greater value to this study in the determination of the unit of measurement of educational need is the per-teacher enrollment in the typical (median) school in each class of communities. The per-teacher enrollment in the typical (median) school in only four of the classes of communities was 31 and in four other classes the per-teacher enrollment in the typical (median) school was 32, while in eight other classes of communities the per-teacher enrollment in the typical (median) school was 33, and in three others the per-teacher enrollment was 34. The median per-teacher enrollment of the medians of the various classes of communities was therefore 33. A study of column two will show that there is great similarity in the average enrollment per teacher in the different sizes of schools, e. g., the schools employing different numbers of teachers. The arithmetic average per-teacher enrollment for each class of communities hovers around 33. The average of the averages is 33. When the total enrollment in the state was divided by the number of teachers employed, the average enrollment was found to be 33.

In the light of the facts shown above, it seems evident that we are justified in drawing the conclusion that in all schools employing two or more teachers an accurate measure of the number of teacher units needed could be determined by dividing the enrollment by 33, the typical per-teacher enrollment. The conclusion, based on the findings of the application of this method, then, is that each county should be allowed one teacher for every one-teacher school regardless of size, and for schools employing two or more teachers the county should be allowed one teacher for every 33 pupils enrolled, and a fraction of a teacher allowance for every fraction of 33 pupils.

The results thus obtained were checked, as presented in the following paragraphs, by the application of the technique developed by Mort.[1] To do this it was necessary to prepare Table III showing the teacher allowance per pupil for schools of various sizes. The number of pupils per teacher is also given in Table III.

---

[1] Paul R. Mort, *The Measurement of Educational Need.* In presenting the application of Dr. Mort's technique to the present problem, it has been deemed unnecessary to define his terms or enter upon an explanation of his formulæ. For these and all other similar matters, the interested reader is referred to Dr. Mort's dissertation, already cited in the present footnote.

TABLE III

TEACHERS PROVIDED FOR EACH PUPIL ENROLLED
IN GEORGIA SCHOOLS

Enrollment	Number of Schools	Average Teachers Per-pupil Enrolled	Average Number Pupils per Teacher
0– 4	1	.3333	3.0000
5– 9	19	.1338	7.474
10– 14	67	.0811	12.329
15– 19	165	.0594	16.832
20– 24	256	.0460	21.734
25– 29	295	.0391	25.605
30– 34	279	.0351	28.504
35– 39	299	.0334	29.970
40– 44	257	.0313	31.896
45– 49	230	.0326	30.687
50– 54	226	.0324	30.843
55– 59	187	.0331	30.240
60– 64	162	.0327	30.596
65– 69	142	.0306	32.653
70– 74	140	.0310	32.259
75– 79	107	.0291	34.310
80– 84	87	.0295	33.873
85– 89	103	.0303	33.015
90– 94	69	.0297	33.670
95– 99	64	.0285	35.077
100–109	105	.0297	33.683
110–119	94	.0289	34.649
120–129	62	.0300	33.375
130–139	106	.0290	34.454
150–174	83	.0303	32.956
175–199	74	.0300	33.260
200–249	117	.0304	32.924
250–299	87	.0290	34.504
300–500	118	.0292	34.262
500–700	63	.0292	34.248
700 and above	30	.0291	34.314

An inspection of Table III shows that the teacher allowance per pupil does not decrease significantly after the enrollment reaches 75. A further inspection raises the question as to whether an enrollment of 40 is not the point above which the teacher allowance per pupil does not decrease significantly. Let us then compare the results of accepting each of these two enrollments as the point above which the teacher allowance per pupil does not decrease significantly. If an enrollment of 40 is accepted, the average teacher allowance per pupil is .0333 (the total number of teachers divided by the enrollment). In this case, the *a*-value is 0, and the *b*-value is .0333. The question then is, would the schools with an enrollment of 40 to 75 be allowed an equal number of teachers by the application of the above *a* and *b* values as they would if the teacher allowance was based on *a* and *b* values derived for this group? This makes it necessary to find the *a* and *b* values for the group, which is done by forming the schools having an enrollment from 40 to 75 inclusive into a table of double entry, showing the distribution of teachers for schools of each size. (See Table IV).

TABLE IV

SCHOOLS HAVING 40 OR MORE BUT LESS THAN 75 PUPILS ENROLLED

Enrollment	Number of Teachers				Total
	1	2	3	4	
40 to 44	170	85	2		257
45 " 49	111	114	5		230
50 " 54	77	145	4		226
55 " 59	35	140	11	1	187
60 " 64	14	130	17	1	162
65 " 69	16	108	17	1	142
70 " 74	5	103	27	5	140
Total	428	825	83	8	1,344

The entries in the body of the table indicate the number of schools with a given enrollment and a given number of teachers. The *a*-value and *b*-value were then obtained by the regression method. The *a*-value, which is the constant term in the equation, was found to be .08; the *b*-value, which represents the slope of the line of best fit, was found to be .0301. It was found that the number of teachers that would be allowed to schools of this group by the use of the *a*(.08) and *b*(.0301) values for this group would be practically the same as would be allowed if the *a*-value of 0 and the *b*-value of .0333 were used. The difference would be still further reduced if the influence of the large schools was eliminated, as was done by Mort[*] for reasons which he stated.

[*] Paul R. Mort, *The Measurement of Educational Need*, p. 26.

From a consideration of the foregoing facts, it appears that little is to be gained by the use of the 75 point, which is more difficult to administer, and not so simple. It seems justifiable therefore to use the 40 point as the point above which there is no significant decrease in the number of teachers per pupil. The a-value is 0 and the b-value is .0333. To find the number of teachers to which a school is entitled, it would be necessary to multiply the b-value (.0333) by the enrollment. The same result would be obtained by dividing the enrollment by 33.256 (the number of pupils per teacher). This is equivalent to saying that every school is entitled to one teacher for every 33.256 pupils or fraction thereof. Under Mort's method, the one-teacher schools were treated separately and one teacher was allowed for each school. This technique as applied to Georgia means that all one-teacher schools, regardless of enrollment, are entitled to one teacher, and that all other schools are entitled to one teacher for every 33.256 pupils, and a proportional additional teacher allowance for any number of pupils in excess of 33.256.

Both techniques used in this chapter for the measurement of educational need arrived at the same conclusion, viz., that one-teacher schools should be treated separately and that one teacher should be provided for every one-teacher school regardless of enrollment, and that the teacher allowance for all other schools should be one teacher for every 33 pupils enrolled, and a proportionate teacher allowance for every additional 33 pupils enrolled or fraction thereof.

As previously noted, enrollment is not so accurate a measure of educational need as average daily attendance. It is therefore recommended that in the future the reports made by county school superintendents to the state department of education indicate the average daily attendance for each school. Until this is done, it is recommended that enrollment be converted or translated into average daily attendance. The average daily attendance for the state as a whole is 75 per cent of the total enrollment. Applying this to the enrollment allowance per teacher (33 pupils), we find that the average daily attendance per teacher would be 25. States more advanced educationally than Georgia and with more wealth [*] have used 30 or more pupils in average daily attendance in determining the number of teacher units needed. Georgia, it seems, could hardly undertake a more ambitious program than these states. It is therefore believed that 30 pupils in average daily attendance should be considered an entirely satisfactory basis for determining the number of teacher units needed, except in one-teacher schools. The plan offered by the present study proposes therefore that one teacher should be provided for all one-teacher schools, and that the teacher allowance for all other schools shall be one teacher for every 30 pupils in average daily attendance, and a proportionate teacher allowance for every additional 33 pupils in average daily attendance or fraction thereof.

We have now completed our determination of the method and the basis for computing the number of teacher units needed. The remainder of the present chapter will be devoted to an application of this technique to the 160 counties comprising the State of Georgia. It is evident that this application is merely a matter of arithmetical computation. It follows that the results can be most clearly and conveniently offered to the reader through tabular presentation. This is done in Table V, which presents in alphabetical order Georgia's 160 counties with the number of teacher units needed computed by the method and on the basis already described.

TABLE V

NUMBER OF TEACHER UNITS NEEDED

County	Teacher Units	County	Teacher Units
Appling	80	Bibb	380
Atkinson	53	Bleckley	62
Bacon	54	Brantley	49
Baker	52	Brooks	147
Baldwin	106	Bryan	51
Banks	86	Bulloch	186
Barrow	105	Burke	143
Barton	150	Butts	66
Ben Hill	97	Calhoun	56
Berrien	125	Camden	47

[*] California and North Carolina are illustrations.

TABLE V.—(Continued)

County	Teacher Units	County	Teacher Units
Campbell	99	Haralson	129
Candler	53	Harris	84
Carroll	219	Hart	119
Catoosa	42	Heard	107
Charlton	44	Henry	117
Chatham	425	Houston	123
Chattahoochee	20	Irwin	89
Chattooga	83	Jackson	151
Cherokee	127	Jasper	89
Clarke	141	Jeff Davis	70
Clay	46	Jefferson	118
Clayton	75	Jenkins	65
Clinch	41	Johnson	100
Cobb	213	Jones	85
Coffee	131	Lamar	56
Colquitt	211	Lanier	35
Columbia	68	Laurens	251
Cook	97	Lee	78
Coweta	193	Liberty	66
Crawford	50	Lincoln	69
Crisp	101	Long	27
Dade	26	Lowndes	178
Dawson	23	Lumpkin	29
Decatur	157	Macon	102
DeKalb	184	Madison	118
Dodge	127	Marion	54
Dooly	127	Meriwether	133
Dougherty	118	Miller	59
Douglas	63	Milton	47
Early	114	Mitchell	147
Echols	24	Monroe	83
Effingham	79	Montgomery	63
Elbert	134	Morgan	97
Emanuel	176	Murray	61
Evans	44	Muscogee	304
Fannin	77	McDuffie	66
Fayette	65	McIntosh	40
Floyd	252	Newton	138
Forsyth	79	Oconse	66
Franklin	126	Oglethorpe	109
Fulton	1711	Paulding	97
Gilmer	62	Pickens	66
Glascock	33	Pierce	79
Glynn	79	Pike	75
Gordon	128	Polk	157
Grady	147	Pulaski	60
Greene	94	Putnam	64
Gwinnette	212	Quitman	18
Habersham	80	Rabun	37
Hale	170	Randolph	92
Hancock	93	Richmond	300

TABLE V.—(Continued)

County	Teacher Units	County	Teacher Units
Rockdale	60	Treutlen	43
Schley	50	Turner	80
Screven	127	Twiggs	57
Seminole	57	Union	36
Spaulding	125	Upson	117
Stephens	82	Walker	141
Stewart	79	Walton	159
Sumter	172	Ware	180
Talbot	57	Warren	84
Taliaferro	56	Washington	150
Tattnall	97	Wayne	81
Taylor	79	Webster	31
Telfair	111	Wheeler	71
Terrell	119	White	39
Thomas	209	Whitfield	119
Tift	78	Wilcox	130
Toombs	93	Wilkes	98
Towns	26	Wilkinson	68
Troup	229	Worth	173

From Table V we see that the total number of teacher units required for the state of Georgia is 18,104. The number of teacher units needed for the respective counties varies all the way from 18 to 1711. It would have been interesting, as well as valuable, to have indicated for each county the number of teacher units to be allowed for one-teacher schools, two-teacher schools, etc. But the limits set to the present account in view of many practical considerations preclude any such detailed presentation. Moreover, those interested in the problem of the present study from a practical standpoint will, except in a very few cases, not care to enter upon any such detailed analysis.

We have now completed our consideration of the first of the two factors entering into a measurement of educational need, viz., the number of teacher units needed. It will be recalled that the second of these factors, as explained in an opening paragraph of the present chapter, is the determination of current expenditure per teacher. This second phase of the problem will be presented in Chapter III.

CHAPTER III

THE COST OF THE EDUCATIONAL OFFERING GEORGIA SHOULD PROVIDE

As stated in the preceding chapter, two elements which may be employed to determine the cost of any educational offering are the number of teacher units needed and the current expenditures per teacher. In Chapter II, the number of teacher units needed by each county was determined. The present chapter will undertake to determine the cost per unit which the state of Georgia can and should equalize. It seems reasonable to propose that it is the duty of the state to provide all the children of the state with an educational opportunity which will include at least such elements as are common to all schools of the state. Obviously, this will not include all school facilities found in those schools providing a more expensive offering. Neither is it proposed here that the state shall assume any responsibility for the purchase of sites, erection of buildings, purchase of additional equipment, or any other items of capital outlay. By educational offering as used in this study is meant that kind of educational opportunity which can be provided with a certain amount of money per teacher unit, viz., the kind of teacher, instructional supplies, supervision, administration, and other items of current expense.[1] What kind of offering should Georgia equalize? What is the per-teacher unit cost required to provide this offering?

In order to determine what amount of money the state of Georgia should provide per teacher unit to guarantee at least a minimum educational opportunity to all its children, it seems reasonable to propose that the average amount of money now spent for current expenses per teacher, or some more representative amount, should be provided to each county for every teacher unit needed. When this is done the state will have equalized to every child in the state an educational opportunity up to the amount provided per teacher unit.

[1] J. R. McGaughy, "The Superintendent's Analysis of School Finances." *Teachers College Record* 26: 386–88. This reference is given for those desiring a more detailed analysis of the items of current expense.

How may we determine the current expense per teacher? In Chapter I, attention was called to the fact that due to the system of accounting and reporting now employed in Georgia, it was impossible to ascertain total current expenses. In view of these facts, the cost of teachers' salaries has been employed as a basis for determining the total current expense per teacher. This procedure is further justified, since the major portion of current expenses is teachers' salaries, and since there is a close relationship between teachers' salaries and current expense, as shown by investigations,[2] and as applied in actual practice by the state of Maryland.[3] Maryland first makes up her salary budget, and then on the basis of this budget calculates her total current expense budget.

Before proceeding further in the present study, it is necessary to determine the average salary per teacher in Georgia in order to get a basis from which may be determined total current expense per teacher. It is possible to determine this average teacher salary by at least two methods. The first and simplest method would consist of dividing the total expenditure for teachers' salaries by the total number of teachers actually employed. The average teacher's salary determined by this method amounted to $567. The method just employed may be objected to on the ground that the result reached might be unduly affected by the salaries paid in the few wealthy counties which employ large numbers of teachers. In order to guard against any such possible error, the average salary was calculated for each county of the state. The county average salaries were then ranked, as shown in Table VI.

[2] George D. Strayer and Robert M. Haig, *The Financing of Education in the State of New York*, p. 43, f.n.l.

[3] *Maryland School Laws*, 1922. In making this computation, Maryland considers that teachers' salaries constitute 76 per cent of total current expenses.

TABLE VI

AN ORDER DISTRIBUTION OF THE AVERAGE SALA-RIES PAID TEACHERS IN THE 160 COUNTIES IN GEORGIA

$1,418	$705	$592	$534	$471
1,397	703	590	534	469
1,292	699	587	531	450
1,279	695	587	530	448
1,226	694	587	527	458
1,205	692	586	526	448
1,069	687	585	525	447
1,057	684 25%	584 5%	523 15%	446
960	679	582	517	441
921	676	581	510	440
890	666	579	509	435
875	660	575	505	428
862	654	569	504	425
832	648	569	500	423
831	641	568	499	420
805	641 20%	567 Median	496 20%	416
786	641	565	492	410
783	637	564	490	408
780	635	563	490	403
777	619 15%	559	489	397
769	632	559	485	385
764	629	559	481	380
752	629	557	480	364
744	627	553 5%	480 25%	352
740	617	551	479	332
735	616	551	479	331
725	612	550	479	326
725	606	549	478	326
718	602	545	475	313
717	593	543	475	306
716	593	541	473	296
715	592 10%	539 10%	472	292

Median salary per teacher for state................$566.50
Average salary for middle 10 per cent.............. 566.88
Average salary for middle 20 per cent.............. 566.78
Average salary for middle 30 per cent.............. 566.63
Average salary per teacher for state.............. 567.00

From Table VI it is seen that the average salary per teacher varies from $1,418 in one county to $292 in another. It is significant that the county paying an average salary of $1,418 per teacher is one of the ten counties having the greatest ability to pay for education (as measured by the tax valuation per teacher), while the county paying an average salary of $292 per teacher is one of the seven counties having the least ability to pay. It is significant also that the eight counties paying the largest average salary per teacher are eight of the ten counties having the greatest ability to pay.

The median salary per teacher, as shown by Table VI, is $567. The average salary for the middle 10 per cent was calculated and found to be $567. The average salaries for the middle 20 per cent and for the middle 30 per cent were also calculated and found to be $567. The average salary for the state, calculated by dividing the total paid for teachers' salaries by the total number of teachers employed in the state, surprising as it may seem, proved to be the same amount, viz., $567 per teacher. In view of these findings, it was decided to use $567 as the salary index for determining the total current expense per teacher.

In order to derive the total current expenses per teacher from the salaries paid teachers in Georgia, it will be necessary to determine what per cent teachers' salaries are of current expenses. As stated in a preceding paragraph, Maryland, in computing total current expenses, considers teachers' salaries as 76 per cent of the same. Morrison concludes that teachers' salaries are more than 80 per cent of the current expenses of schools in North Carolina.[4] McGaughy made a study of school costs in 50 southern cities having a population of 8,000 or more up to 100,-000. He found in those cities that teachers' salaries were 75 per cent of current expenses.[5]

In many of the small schools of Georgia, the janitorial service and fuel costs, together with certain other costs, are very small. The pupils, under the direction of the teacher, clean the buildings and grounds, and fuel is frequently supplied by the trustees or other persons interested in the school. In view of these and other considerations, it appears entirely justifiable to draw the conclusion that teachers' salaries are 80 per cent of all current expenses in Georgia. On this basis, then, accepting the salary index determined above, viz., $567 as 80 per cent of the average current expense per teacher, $700 may be justified as the average total current expense per teacher.[6] Hereafter, $700 will be re-

[4] F. W. Morrison. Unpublished Ph.D. Thesis.
[5] J. R. McGaughy, *The Fiscal Administration of City School Systems*, p. 5.
[6] As is evident, the exact amount of average total current expense per teacher, as determined by the present method, is $708.75. For practical considerations, it was deemed advisable to use the approximate figure, $700.

ferred to as the average educational offering for the state. If the state is to provide for every child an educational opportunity equal to the average educational offering for the state, she must equalize $700 per teacher unit in every county in the state. And if the state should equalize this average $700 educational offering, it would require solely for that portion to be supplied by the state (see Table VII) an annual state appropriation of $9,416,-666.[7] While this is the annual appropriation which the state must make before it can claim to equalize educational opportunity and burden of support up to the average for the state, it is not believed that the people of the state will be willing to provide so large a state fund at this time. Table VII shows what must be provided from state sources to equalize the educational offerings costing $700, $600, $500 and $400 per-teacher unit.

TABLE VII

COST OF VARIOUS OFFERINGS AND
SOURCES OF SUPPORT

Offering	Uniform Local Tax Rate in Mills	Cost of Minimum Program	Amount to be Raised by Uniform Local Tax Rate	Amount To Be Raised by the State
$700	2.75	$12,675,600	$3,258,934	$9,416,666
600	2.1	10,862,400	2,488,637	8,373,763
500	1.45	9,054,000	1,722,189	7,331,811
400	.8	7,241,600	936,201	6,305,399

Reserving for a subsequent paragraph final consideration of Table VII, attention is now directed to the data in the first and last columns of this table.

The last column of Table VII shows the amount that must be supplied by the state to equalize an educational offering costing per teacher unit the amount set opposite it in column one. Georgia is now distributing $4,000,000 to the counties of the state. It is evident from the facts presented elsewhere in this and in other chapters that she is equalizing neither educational opportunity nor burden of support. If she should undertake to equalize such an educational offering as could be provided

[7] The method of determining the cost to the state will be explained in a later chapter.

with $400 per teacher unit, it would require a state fund of $6,-305,399. It seems that if she is to attack the problem of equalization at all, she cannot do less than equalize a $400 offering. It is therefore proposed that the minimum educational offering which the state of Georgia can afford to equalize, and to which no defensible objection can be raised, is such an offering as can be made available with $400 per teacher unit. Such an offering will hereafter be referred to as the *minimum educational offering* proposed in this study, a term which must be carefully distinguished from the term, *average educational offering,* already employed to indicate a per-teacher offering of $700.

In order to ascertain the cost of providing this minimum offering in each of the 160 counties in Georgia, the number of teacher units needed in each county, as determined in Chapter II, were multiplied by $400. The costs thus obtained were tabulated by counties and are presented in tabular form in Table VIII.

TABLE VIII

COST OF MINIMUM EDUCATIONAL OFFERING ON
$400 BASIS

County	Number of Teacher Units Needed	Cost of Minimum Educational Offering
Appling	80	$32,000
Atkinson	53	21,200
Bacon	54	21,600
Baker	52	20,800
Baldwin	106	42,400
Banks	86	34,400
Barrow	105	42,000
Bartow	150	60,000
Ben Hill	97	38,800
Berrien	125	50,000
Bibb	380	152,000
Bleckley	62	24,800
Brantley	49	19,600
Brooks	147	58,800
Bryan	51	20,400
Bulloch	186	74,400
Burke	143	57,200
Butts	66	26,400
Calhoun	56	22,400
Camden	47	18,800

TABLE VIII (Cont'd)

County	Number of Teacher Units Needed	Cost of Minimum Educational Offering
Campbell	99	39,600
Candler	53	21,200
Carroll	219	87,600
Catoosa	42	16,800
Charlton	44	17,600
Chatham	425	170,000
Chattahoochee	20	8,000
Chattooga	83	33,200
Cherokee	127	50,800
Clarke	141	56,400
Clay	46	18,400
Clayton	75	30,000
Clinch	41	16,400
Cobb	213	85,200
Coffee	131	52,400
Colquitt	211	84,400
Columbia	68	27,200
Cook	97	38,800
Coweta	193	77,200
Crawford	26	20,000
Crisp	50	40,400
Dade	101	10,400
Dawson	23	9,200
Decatur	157	62,800
DeKalb	184	73,600
Dodge	127	50,800
Dooly	127	50,800
Dougherty	118	47,200
Douglas	63	25,200
Early	114	45,600
Echols	24	9,600
Effingham	79	31,600
Elbert	134	53,600
Emanuel	176	70,400
Evans	44	17,600
Fannin	77	30,800
Fayette	65	26,000
Floyd	252	100,800
Forsythe	79	31,600
Franklin	126	50,400
Fulton	711	684,400
Gilmer	62	24,800
Glascock	33	13,200
Glynn	79	31,600
Gordon	128	51,200
Grady	147	58,800
Greene	94	37,600
Gwinnette	212	84,800
Habersham	80	32,000
Hale	170	68,000

TABLE VIII (Cont'd)

County	Number of Teacher Units Needed	Cost of Minimum Educational Offering
Hancock	93	37,200
Haralson	129	51,600
Harris	84	33,600
Hart	119	47,600
Heard	107	42,800
Henry	117	46,800
Houston	123	49,200
Irwin	89	35,600
Jackson	151	60,400
Jasper	89	35,600
Jeff Davis	70	28,000
Jefferson	118	47,200
Jenkins	65	26,000
Johnson	100	40,000
Jones	85	34,000
Lamar	56	22,400
Lanier	35	14,000
Laurens	251	100,400
Lee	78	31,200
Liberty	66	26,400
Lincoln	69	27,600
Long	27	10,800
Lowndes	178	71,200
Lumpkin	29	11,600
Macon	102	40,800
Madison	118	47,200
Marion	54	21,600
Meriwether	133	53,200
Miller	59	23,600
Milton	47	18,800
Mitchell	147	58,800
Monroe	83	33,200
Montgomery	63	25,200
Morgan	97	38,800
Murray	61	24,400
Muscogee	304	121,600
McDuffie	66	26,400
McIntosh	40	26,400
Newton	138	16,000
Oconee	66	55,200
Oglethorpe	109	43,600
Paulding	97	38,800
Pickens	66	26,400
Pierce	79	31,600
Pike	75	30,000
Polk	157	62,800
Pulaski	60	24,000
Putnam	64	25,600
Quitman	18	7,200
Rabun	37	14,800

TABLE VIII (Cont'd)

County	Number of Teacher Units Needed	Cost of Minimum Educational Offering
Randolph	92	36,800
Richmond	300	120,000
Rockdale	60	24,000
Schley	50	20,000
Screven	127	50,800
Seminole	57	22,800
Spaulding	125	50,000
Stephens	82	32,800
Stewart	79	31,600
Sumter	172	68,800
Talbot	57	22,800
Taliaferro	56	22,400
Tattnall	97	38,800
Taylor	79	31,600
Telfair	111	44,400
Terrell	119	47,600
Thomas	209	83,600
Tift	78	31,200
Toombs	93	37,200
Towns	26	10,400
Trout	229	91,600
Treutlen	43	17,200
Turner	80	32,000
Twiggs	57	22,800
Union	36	14,400
Upson	117	46,800
Walker	141	56,400
Walton	159	63,600
Ware	180	72,000
Warren	84	33,600
Washington	150	60,000
Wayne	81	32,400
Webster	31	12,400
Wheeler	71	28,400
White	39	15,600
Whitfield	119	47,600
Wilcox	130	52,000
Wilkes	98	39,200
Wilkinson	68	27,200
Worth	173	69,200

Similar cost data were prepared and tabulated for the average ($700) educational offering, and for the $500 educational offering, but it was not thought necessary to present them in this study.

Having determined the cost of providing the proposed minimum educational offering in each of the 160 counties of Georgia by the methods explained in the present chapter, it is now important to know the relative ability of the counties to support the minimum program for their county. Chapter IV will be devoted to the determination of a method for measuring the ability of the various counties and to the application of this method.

CHAPTER IV

RELATIVE ABILITY OF VARIOUS COUNTIES TO SUPPORT EDUCATION

The derivation of an adequate method of determining the tax-paying ability of the various counties in Georgia is a necessary prerequisite to the "equalization of educational opportunity" or the "equalization of school support" on a state-wide basis. In Massachusetts approximately 90 per cent of public school revenues are derived from local general property taxes. The largest single source of state revenue is a state income tax. According to a somewhat unusual system, Massachusetts uses approximately one-fifth of the proceeds of the state income tax for state purposes and returns the remaining four-fifths to the towns and cities in proportion to the amount each furnishes. Swift [1] proposed the following as a measure of relative ability to provide school revenue in Massachusetts: The sum of (1) the proceeds per pupil derived from a uniform tax levy, and (2) the income tax payment per pupil. A single illustration will make clear his method. The ability of Nantucket, Massachusetts, to provide school revenue is $106. This figure was derived in the following manner: The total tax valuation was divided by the number of pupils in net average membership and this valuation was multiplied by the average local school tax rate for Massachusetts, which was 7.67 mills. The result of this computation was $95.86. To this amount was added the income tax payment per pupil, which was $10.08, making a total of $105.94. Swift considers that this amount represents in a fairly accurate way the financial ability of Nantucket in comparison with that of other cities and towns of the state. There are three important elements involved here in determining Nantucket's ability to pay. The first is its need expressed in pupil units.[2] The second is the revenue raised by levying the average state-wide tax rate of 7.67 mills on tax valuations, which, in the

---

[1] F. H. Swift, *Studies in Public School Finance. The East*, pp. 97 ff.
[2] Dr. Swift states that the teacher unit is equally acceptable and for purposes of state administration has some advantages over the pupil unit.

case of Massachusetts, are commonly accepted as true valuations. The third is the income tax payment per pupil.

Strayer and Haig[3] employed an index of economic resources and the need expressed in teacher units[4] to determine the relative ability of counties of the state of New York to finance their schools. The index of economic resources, as computed by Strayer and Haig, is a combination of real estate values and income which assigns to a dollar of income ten times the importance given to a dollar of real estate value. The three important elements involved in this method of determining the ability of the counties of the state of New York to finance schools are: (1) Real estate values, (2) taxable income, and (3) the need expressed in teacher units.

It is obvious that of two counties having equal property values per teacher, but one of which has twice or three times as much taxable income per teacher as the other, the ability to support schools of the one which has the larger taxable per teacher income is the greater. It follows then that the most adequate method of supporting education must include a combination of property and income.

In the case of Georgia, an effort was made to get from the United States Commissioner of Internal Revenue the taxable income and the income tax payments for each county in the state of Georgia. Neither could be obtained. And as the state of Georgia does not levy an income tax, no information regarding incomes by counties was available. This may not be such a handicap in deriving a method for the determination of the ability of the counties in Georgia to support education as it at first appears, since incomes are usually considered sources of revenue for the state and the nation, and are also usually considered as impracticable as sources for county revenue. McGaughy[5] maintains in a recent article that the property tax will continue to be the principal source of school money and that "therefore it does not seem valid to compare the relative ability of two communities to pay for education on a basis of a com-

---

[3] George D. Strayer and Robert M. Haig, *The Financing of Education in the State of New York*, Chap. XII.

[4] Other units were used also, viz., average daily attendance, and child of school age.

[5] J. R. McGaughy, "The Superintendent's Analysis of School Finances," *Teachers College Record*, 26: 391–392, January, 1925.

bination of income earned and property owned if school moneys are to be secured through a levy on property alone." It might be added that if incomes are adequately taxed by both state and national governments, it would be unfair to levy a county income tax or to consider income as an element of ability of a county to support education.

The source of local revenue that must be relied upon for the support of education in the counties of Georgia is general property. General property is composed of real, personal and corporate property, all of which yields a significant revenue for local school support. Any method of measuring ability to support schools in Georgia, if it is to be capable of application to conditions as they are, must be based on the present sources of revenue.

In consideration of the above facts just presented and of other significant factors, it was decided to employ as a method for measuring the ability of the counties to support education the relationship that exists between the assessed and equalized property valuation and the number of teacher units needed, e.g., the assessed and equalized valuation per teacher. It is recognized at the outset that this is not an adequate measure of the true or real ability of the counties to support schools, since property in Georgia is actually equalized at 35 per cent of real value [6] instead of 100 per cent as required by law. For the purpose of comparing counties to determine their relative ability to support schools, however, it is considered quite satisfactory, especially since all valuations were equalized at the same rate. In other words, all property in every county of the state is equalized at 35 per cent of its true value and consequently is acceptable as a basis for the determination of the relative ability of the various counties to support schools. The true or real value could have been ascertained with a practical degree of accuracy by multiplying the assessed and equalized values by three. As a basis for a plan of school support, however, real values would not have been usable as revenues under the present system which must be based upon the equalized and assessed values which are usually spoken of as taxable values. More-

[6] *Annual Report* of H. J. Fullbright, State Tax Commissioner of Georgia, for the year 1919, p. 8.

over, it will be recalled that the determination of the ability of the counties is just a step in the general plan of determining how equalization of support can be best achieved under the present system of taxation.

It appears that this method embodies more of the elements that are to be desired in measuring the ability of the counties of Georgia to support education than any other method that could be employed. It also seems that this method lends itself more nearly than any other to the realization of the purpose of this study, viz., the equalization of school support throughout the state.

In order to apply the proposed method of measuring ability, it was necessary to ascertain the total taxable values for each county and divide the taxable value for each county by the number of teacher units needed by each county as determined in Chapter II. The results of the application of the proposed method in determining the ability of the several counties of the state of Georgia can best be presented and comprehended in tabular form. These results are presented in Table IX.

TABLE IX

RELATIVE ABILITY OF COUNTIES TO SUPPORT THEIR EDUCATIONAL PROGRAM

County	Assessed Taxable Value	Number of Teacher Units Needed	Assessed Taxable Value Per-Teacher Unit
Appling	$4,271,019	80	$53,388
Atkinson	2,256,304	53	42,572
Bacon	2,049,923	54	37,962
Baker	1,658,743	52	31,899
Baldwin	4,553,301	106	42,956
Banks	1,935,430	86	22,505
Barrow	3,508,586	105	33,415
Bartow	8,288,248	150	55,255
Ben Hill	4,412,668	97	45,491
Berrien	4,520,031	125	36,169
Bibb	53,744,647	380	141,433
Bleckley	3,279,795	62	52,900
Brantley	2,794,139	49	57,023
Brooks	7,902,497	147	53,758
Bryan	2,383,920	51	46,744
Bulloch	8,311,428	186	44,685

TABLE IX (Cont'd)

County	Assessed Taxable Value	Number of Teacher Units Needed	Assessed Taxable Value Per-Teacher Unit
Burke	9,194,527	143	64,297
Butts	3,423,925	66	51,878
Calhoun	2,629,343	56	46,953
Camden	3,095,287	47	65,857
Campbell	4,161,731	99	42,038
Candler	2,197,982	53	41,471
Carroll	8,460,246	219	38,631
Catoosa	2,077,187	42	49,457
Charlton	2,719,643	44	61,810
Chatham	62,212,001	425	146,381
Chattahoochee	1,082,954	20	54,148
Chattooga	4,772,107	83	57,495
Cherokee	6,551,505	127	51,587
Clarke	20,145,722	141	142,877
Clay	1,823,757	46	39,647
Clayton	3,220,193	75	42,936
Clinch	3,475,689	41	84,773
Cobb	11,415,568	213	53,594
Coffee	5,029,532	131	38,393
Colquitt	8,210,973	211	38,915
Columbia	2,704,320	68	39,769
Cook	3,553,233	97	36,631
Coweta	10,293,108	193	53,332
Crawford	2,063,865	50	41,277
Crisp	5,954,410	101	58,955
Dade	2,427,116	26	93,351
Dawson	646,967	23	28,129
Decatur	8,947,539	157	56,991
DeKalb	25,336,797	184	137,700
Dodge	6,851,391	127	53,948
Dooly	5,253,032	127	41,362
Dougherty	14,807,408	118	125,487
Douglas	2,755,136	63	43,732
Early	5,855,542	114	51,364
Echols	1,504,828	24	62,701
Effingham	4,864,635	79	61,578
Elbert	5,913,846	134	44,133
Emanuel	6,308,845	176	35,846
Evans	1,960,032	44	44,546
Fannin	2,405,461	77	31,240
Fayette	2,013,473	65	30,977
Floyd	21,021,987	252	83,421
Forsyth	1,901,290	79	24,067
Franklin	3,691,719	126	29,299
Fulton	231,503,348	1,711	135,303
Gilmer	1,766,149	62	28,486
Glascock	893,622	33	27,079
Glynn	11,937,181	79	151,104
Gordon	4,958,537	128	38,739

TABLE IX (Cont'd)

County	Assessed Taxable Value	Number of Teacher Units Needed	Assessed Taxable Value Per-Teacher Unit
Grady	4,815,465	147	32,758
Greene	3,992,525	94	42,474
Gwinnett	8,460,483	212	39,908
Habersham	6,012,897	80	75,161
Hall	11,061,224	170	65,066
Hancock	3,448,415	93	37,080
Haralson	3,859,534	129	29,919
Harris	3,997,961	84	47,595
Hart	2,849,403	119	23,945
Heard	1,465,138	107	13,693
Henry	4,749,823	117	40,597
Houston	6,908,219	123	56,164
Irwin	3,104,073	89	34,877
Jackson	5,698,229	151	37,737
Jasper	3,102,379	89	34,858
Jeff Davis	2,302,427	70	32,892
Jefferson	6,178,880	118	52,363
Jenkins	3,560,312	65	54,774
Johnson	2,889,139	100	28,891
Jones	2,755,528	85	32,418
Lamar	3,676,560	56	65,653
Lanier	1,584,995	35	45,286
Laurens	11,871,216	251	47,296
Lee	2,447,663	78	31,380
Liberty	2,782,212	66	42,155
Lincoln	1,616,232	69	23,424
Long	1,928,172	27	71,414
Lowndes	13,939,443	178	78,311
Lumpkin	1,404,743	29	48,439
Macon	4,935,858	102	48,391
Madison	3,442,086	118	29,170
Marion	2,998,651	54	55,531
Meriwether	6,362,456	133	47,838
Miller	2,118,904	59	35,914
Milton	1,372,467	47	29,201
Mitchell	7,097,644	147	48,283
Monroe	5,203,338	83	62,691
Morgan	4,555,807	97	46,967
Murray	3,040,839	61	49,850
Montgomery	2,158,794	63	34,267
Muscogee	41,743,367	304	137,313
McDuffie	2,671,405	66	40,476
McIntosh	1,629,380	40	40,735
Newton	5,335,198	138	38,661
Oconee	2,600,210	66	39,397
Oglethorpe	4,072,508	109	37,362
Paulding	3,611,148	97	37,228
Pickens	2,013,298	66	30,505

TABLE IX (Cont'd)

County	Assessed Taxable Value	Number of Teacher Units Needed	Assessed Taxable Value Per- Teacher Unit
Pierce	3,672,546	79	46,488
Pike	2,514,061	75	33,521
Polk	8,877,557	157	56,545
Pulaski	3,451,876	60	57,531
Putnam	2,682,439	64	41,913
Quitman	969,814	18	53,879
Rabun	2,564,057	37	69,299
Randolph	3,947,807	92	42,911
Richmond	46,015,845	300	153,386
Rockdale	2,322,056	60	38,701
Schley	1,711,239	50	34,225
Screven	5,224,740	127	41,140
Seminole	2,451,639	57	43,011
Spalding	8,613,757	125	68,910
Stephens	3,411,140	82	41,599
Stewart	4,062,013	79	51,418
Sumter	10,377,726	172	60,335
Talbot	2,331,871	57	40,910
Taliaferro	1,675,456	56	29,919
Tattnall	4,287,346	97	44,199
Taylor	2,472,681	79	31,300
Telfair	5,115,325	111	46,084
Terrell	4,598,814	119	38,645
Thomas	13,240,223	209	63,350
Tift	5,618,720	78	72,035
Toombs	4,802,293	93	51,638
Towns	783,220	26	30,124
Troup	14,170,943	229	61,882
Treutlen	1,797,268	43	41,797
Turner	3,456,774	80	43,210
Twiggs	2,287,986	57	40,140
Union	949,760	36	26,382
Upson	4,872,206	117	41,643
Walker	8,035,797	141	56,991
Walton	5,009,681	159	31,507
Ware	11,508,866	180	63,938
Warren	2,406,253	84	28,646
Washington	7,216,982	150	48,113
Wayne	5,728,745	81	70,725
Webster	1,621,377	31	52,303
Wheeler	2,324,241	71	32,736
White	1,537,430	39	39,421
Whitfield	7,489,957	119	62,940
Wilcox	3,858,024	130	29,677
Wilkes	5,901,469	98	60,219
Wilkinson	10,251,379	68	150,755
Worth	5,551,289	173	32,088

Even a cursory consideration of the inequalities in the ability of the various counties of Georgia to support schools as revealed in Table IX shows the utter futility of expecting any system which derives its revenues from county sources ever to produce equality of educational funds and consequently equality of educational opportunity. The county of greatest ability has a valuation of $153,386 per teacher. The county of least ability has a valuation of only $13,693 per teacher. In other words, the most able county is 11.2 times as able to support schools as the county of least ability. The county of median ability has a valuation of $44,166 per teacher. This median county has less than one-third the ability to pay that the county of greatest ability has.

A table was prepared showing the counties arranged in the order of their ability from the highest to the lowest, but it was not considered necessary to include it in the present account in view of the fact that the same information is made available in Table IX, although not in the same form.

Conditions revealed in the present chapter demand that attention be called to the necessity of at least two important tax reforms, despite the fact that it does not lie within the scope of this study to propose methods for carrying out these recommendations. The two recommendations are:

1. That a more scientific method of assessment be employed and that real or true values be made the basis of taxation.
2. That a more adequate and equitable system of taxation be inaugurated which will tap all sources of revenue and provide that the burden of taxation be distributed equally in proportion to ability to pay, making it possible for every community to provide as good schools as it may desire.

The relative ability of every county in Georgia has been determined by the method developed in this chapter. This is the third problem that it was necessary to solve in order that it might be used as a basis for the scientific determination of a plan of state support of schools in Georgia.

In Chapter V, a plan for the support of public schools in Georgia will be determined and an application of the plan will be made to the minimum educational offering for the state.

CHAPTER V

A PLAN OF SCHOOL SUPPORT FOR GEORGIA

The plan of school support for Georgia presented in the present study has two major purposes: (1) the provision of a minimum educational offering for every child within the state; (2) the distribution of the burden of support of such offering so that it will bear equally upon all in proportion to their ability. Any such plan must take into consideration both the great differences in the ability of the various counties, revealed in the preceding chapter, and also the effects of the operation of the present system of distributing the state school fund.

The State School Fund. The evils resulting from the present method of apportionment which employs the census child as the unit for distribution of the state school fund were shown in Chapter II. An evil of even greater significance, not dealt with in Chapter II, affecting both the equalization of educational opportunity and the equalization of school support is to be found in the fact that the present method of distributing the state fund does not take into consideration the ability of the various counties to support their schools. The present system of distributing the state school fund gives the same amount of state aid per child to the wealthiest county in the state as to the poorest. The great existing inequalities in the educational opportunities in the wealthy and the poor counties are sufficient basis for condemning the present system of distribution as an instrument of equalization. Under the present system, as shown in Chapter III, eight of the ten wealthiest counties pay the largest salaries to teachers and consequently secure teachers with superior experience and training.[1] Comparisons with regard to length of term, buildings, equipment, libraries, etc., would reveal further the fact that the present system of state aid not only fails to produce equality of opportunity but actually creates and aggravates inequalities. Under the present system of distribution, equality of opportunity not only does not exist but cannot exist

[1] For experience and training of teachers, see *State School Survey*, 1923.

even though the poorer counties levy taxes far heavier than those now levied by the wealthier. The force of these statements will be evident from a comparison of Richmond, the richest county in the state, with Heard, the poorest county.

Under the present system of state aid, it would be necessary for Richmond County to make a levy of only 1.6 mills[2] on equalized valuation in order to provide the minimum $400 educational offering proposed in Chapter III, whereas Heard County would be forced to levy on equalized valuation 17.6 mills[3] in order to provide the same offering. Under the present system of state aid, both counties would receive approximately $150 per teacher from the state, and in order to provide $400 per teacher, it would be necessary for each to raise $250 per teacher. Richmond County could do this by a levy of 1.6 mills, whereas Heard County would be obliged to levy 17.6 mills. At the present time, Heard County is employing only 65 teachers,[4] whereas she needs 107.[5] Richmond County, on the other hand, is employing 316 teachers,[6] which is 16 teachers more than would be required on the basis of 30 pupils in average daily attendance per teacher. Equalization of educational opportunity will never be achieved in Georgia until the present system of distributing the state school fund is abandoned.

It will be well to consider briefly at this point certain outstanding systems of policies of school support. Of such there are three general, rather all-inclusive, types, viz., (1) local support, i.e., systems in which by far the major portion of school revenues are furnished by local units, counties, towns, or school districts, (2) complete state support, and (3) a combination of local and state support.

Local Support. In 1920, only three states in the union, Alabama, Texas and Mississippi, derived more than 50 per cent of their total public school revenues from state funds, whereas fourteen states derived less than 10 per cent. The present paragraph is concerned not only with states in which state funds provide a relatively small—in many cases, a negligible—portion

---

[2] Approximate.
[3] Approximate.
[4] *Annual Report,* 1922, Georgia Department of Education, Tables 1 and 9.
[5] See above, Table V, p. 25.
[6] See footnote 4.

of the total school revenue, but with states in which such state aid as is provided is not distributed in a manner to produce among the local units equalization of school revenues, school burdens, and educational opportunities. Equalization under such systems will always remain impossible, owing to the great inequalities in the financial ability of the various local units, whether such units be school districts as in the majority of our states, towns as in New England, counties as in Georgia and in other southern states.

Complete State Support. By complete state school support is meant a system whereby the state supplies all the revenue and administers the schools. Here we have complete centralized school support and control. Delaware most nearly approaches this type. The state assumes entire support for the minimum offering required of every community. Here equalization of opportunity and equalization of support are carried to their logical conclusions, viz., revenues are provided chiefly from a state income tax and the required minimum offering is guaranteed for every child at the expense of the state. This has been referred to as the large fund method. It is contended by those opposed to this plan of school support that the interest of the community is lost, that local initiative with its consequent variation and experimentation is sacrificed to a deadening uniformity and that the state's greatest agency for creating an interest in and training for citizenship fails. Supporters of the policy of complete state support are ready with answers to each of these objections, but it lies outside the scope of the present study to attempt an evaluation of the merits of the case. Were Georgia to adopt this method, a complete reorganization of the tax system of the state would be required, with its attendant difficulties. The great advantages of this system are recognized, but it is doubtful if public opinion in Georgia would accept a solution on this basis. Let us turn then to a combination of state and local support.

Combination of State and Local Support. This is the method employed by most of our states.[7] There are many combinations of state and local support in the United States which do not equalize educational opportunity of even a minimum offering.

[7] See State School Codes of different states.

Georgia's system, as pointed out in the pages of the present chapter, is one of these.

Of those states employing this method, Maryland has most effectively applied the principle of equalization. She requires that each county levy a 6.7 mill tax on a state-wide equalized assessment. The state then provides the additional funds required to maintain the minimum offering.[8] This method of school support has been referred to as the small fund method, since it is necessary for the state to provide a much smaller fund by combination method than by the complete support or large fund method. Other states which are distributing state school funds, in part at least, as equalization funds, are Maine, New Hampshire, Pennsylvania, California, Colorado and Minnesota.[9]

In determining and proposing a plan of school support for Georgia, it is well to bear in mind that the citizenship of Georgia has never relinquished the responsibility accepted by its forefathers, for the principle of providing equality of educational opportunity and equality of school support. Never since this principle was written into the Constitution of 1776, and later into the present constitution, has there been such an insistent demand for its realization as to-day. Never has there been such a complete lack of its realization as to-day. It remains to be seen whether the economic adjustments required in order to produce equalization of educational opportunity will dispel the enthusiasm for its realization.

The Proposed Plan. The essential elements of the system of school support for Georgia about to be proposed with a view of insuring equalization would require (1) that every county levy a uniform tax to provide its contribution to the minimum offering on equalized valuation; (2) that the amount of this tax rate be determined by the tax rate it would be necessary for the wealthiest county in the state to levy in order to provide the minimum educational offering the state agrees to equalize; (3) that the state supply the difference between the amount thus raised by each county and the total amount necessary to finance the minimum offering; (4) that the state set up administrative

[8] See *Maryland School Laws*, 1922.
[9] F. H. Swift, *A Biennial Survey of Public School Finance in the United States*, 1920-22, pp. 19-25.

conditions for participation in the state fund which will (*a*) provide adequate information for the accurate determination of the state's financial responsibility, and (*b*) insure economical expenditure of all funds necessary to provide the minimum offering the state assumes to equalize. These elements, together with one other proposed in the following paragraph, are accepted as the elements of the proposed plan of school support for Georgia.

The elements presented in the preceding paragraph will be modified only in so far as it is necessary to protect every county against receiving from the state a sum less than it now receives. This departure from the principles is necessary in view of the fact that counties which have been receiving funds from the state have come to look upon receiving these funds as a vested right, and have made their program of development with the expectation that they would receive this aid. These facts, together with other practical considerations, justify the exception.

The first step in working out the plan here proposed was to determine the tax rate necessary for the wealthiest (Richmond) county to levy in order to support the minimum ($400) offering per teacher proposed in Chapter III. Table VIII shows the total cost to Richmond County of providing the offering, and the tax rate, .8 mills, is the rate she must levy to support the minimum offering after the amount she receives from the state has been deducted. Since the uniform local tax rate is determined by the tax rate which the wealthiest county must levy in order to provide the minimum educational offering, the uniform local tax rate that every county must levy in order to participate in the state fund is .8 mills. Table VII, column two, shows the uniform local tax rates that every county would be required to levy for the various offerings costing the amount per teacher shown in column one of the table. Column three shows the total cost of providing the minimum and other offerings, while column four shows the total amount to be raised by the uniform local tax and column five the total amount it would be necessary for the state to provide under the proposed plan.

Column one, Table X, shows the total cost of providing the minimum offering in every county in the state. This total cost for the different counties was determined as explained in Chapter III.

TABLE X

COST OF MINIMUM EDUCATIONAL OFFERING AND SOURCES OF ITS SUPPORT

(Based on $400 Per-Teacher Unit)

County	Cost of Minimum Program	Amount Raised by Uniform Local Tax	Amount Supplied by State
Appling	$32,000	$3,417	$28,583
Atkinson	21,200	1,805	19,395
Bacon	21,600	1,640	19,960
Baker	20,800	1,327	19,473
Baldwin	42,400	3,642	38,758
Banks	34,400	1,548	32,852
Barrow	42,000	2,807	39,193
Bartow	60,000	6,630	53,370
Ben Hill	38,800	3,530	35,270
Berrien	50,000	3,616	46,384
Bibb	152,000	42,996	109,004
Bleckley	24,800	2,624	22,176
Brantley	19,600	2,235	17,365
Brooks	58,800	60,322	52,478
Bryan	20,400	1,907	18,493
Bulloch	74,400	6,649	67,751
Burke	57,200	7,356	49,844
Butts	26,400	2,739	23,661
Calhoun	22,400	2,103	20,297
Camden	18,800	2,476	16,324
Campbell	39,600	3,330	36,270
Candler	21,200	1,758	19,442
Carroll	87,600	6,768	80,832
Catoosa	16,800	1,662	15,138
Charlton	17,600	2,176	15,424
Chatham	170,000	49,770	120,230
Chattahoochee	8,000	866	7,134
Chattooga	33,200	3,818	29,382
Cherokee	50,800	5,242	45,558
Clarke	56,400	16,117	40,283
Clay	18,400	1,459	16,941
Clayton	30,000	2,576	27,424
Clinch	16,400	2,781	13,619
Cobb	85,200	9,132	76,068
Coffee	52,400	4,024	48,376
Colquitt	84,400	6,569	77,831
Columbia	27,200	2,163	25,037
Cook	38,800	2,842	35,958
Coweta	77,200	8,234	68,966
Crawford	20,000	1,651	18,349
Crisp	40,400	4,763	35,637
Dade	10,400	1,942	8,458
Dawson	9,200	518	8,682

TABLE X (Cont'd)

County	Cost of Minimum Program	Amount Raised by Uniform Local Tax	Amount Supplied by State
Decatur	62,800	7,158	55,642
DeKalb	73,600	20,270	53,330
Dodge	50,800	5,481	45,319
Dooly	50,800	4,202	46,598
Dougherty	47,200	11,846	35,354
Douglas	25,200	2,204	22,996
Early	45,600	4,685	40,915
Echols	9,600	1,204	8,396
Effingham	31,600	3,892	27,708
Elbert	53,600	4,731	48,869
Emanuel	70,400	5,047	65,353
Evans	17,600	1,568	16,032
Fannin	30,800	1,924	28,876
Fayette	26,000	1,610	24,390
Floyd	100,800	16,818	83,982
Forsyth	31,600	1,521	30,079
Franklin	50,400	2,954	47,446
Fulton	684,400	185,202	499,198
Gilmer	24,800	1,413	23,387
Glascock	13,200	715	12,485
Glynn	31,600	9,550	22,050
Gordon	51,200	3,967	47,233
Grady	58,800	3,852	54,948
Greene	37,600	3,194	34,406
Gwinnett	84,800	6,768	78,032
Habersham	32,000	4,810	27,190
Hall	68,000	8,849	59,151
Hancock	37,200	2,758	34,442
Haralson	51,600	3,088	48,512
Harris	33,600	3,198	30,402
Hart	47,600	2,279	45,321
Heard	42,800	1,172	41,628
Henry	46,800	3,800	43,000
Houston	49,200	5,526	43,674
Irwin	35,600	2,483	33,117
Jackson	60,400	4,558	55,842
Jasper	35,600	2,482	33,118
Jeff Davis	28,000	1,842	26,158
Jefferson	47,200	4,943	42,257
Jenkins	26,000	2,848	23,152
Johnson	40,000	2,311	37,689
Jones	34,000	2,205	31,795
Lamar	22,400	2,942	19,458
Lanier	14,000	1,268	12,732
Laurens	100,400	9,497	90,903
Lee	31,200	1,958	29,242
Liberty	26,400	2,226	24,174
Lincoln	27,600	1,293	26,307
Long	10,800	1,542	9,258

TABLE X (Cont'd)

County	Cost of Minimum Program	Amount Raised by Uniform Local Tax	Amount Supplied by State
Lowndes	71,200	11,151	60,049
Lumpkin	11,600	1,124	10,476
Macon	40,800	3,949	36,851
Madison	47,200	2,754	44,446
Marion	21,600	2,399	19,201
Meriwether	53,200	5,090	48,110
Miller	23,600	1,695	21,905
Milton	18,800	1,098	17,702
Mitchell	58,800	5,678	53,122
Monroe	33,200	4,162	29,038
Montgomery	25,200	1,727	23,473
Morgan	38,800	3,645	35,155
Murray	24,400	2,433	21,967
Muscogee	121,600	33,394	88,206
McDuffie	26,400	2,137	24,263
McIntosh	16,000	1,303	14,697
Newton	55,200	4,268	50,932
Oconee	26,400	2,080	24,320
Oglethorpe	43,600	3,258	40,342
Paulding	38,800	2,889	35,911
Pickens	26,400	1,610	24,790
Pierce	31,600	2,938	28,662
Pike	30,000	2,011	27,989
Polk	62,800	7,102	55,698
Pulaski	24,000	2,762	21,238
Putnam	25,600	2,146	23,454
Quitman	7,200	776	6,424
Rabun	14,800	2,051	12,749
Randolph	36,800	3,158	33,642
Richmond	120,000	36,813	83,187
Rockdale	24,000	1,858	22,142
Schley	20,000	1,369	18,631
Screven	50,800	4,180	46,620
Seminole	22,800	1,962	20,838
Spaulding	50,000	6,891	43,109
Stephens	32,800	2,729	30,071
Stewart	31,600	3,250	28,350
Sumter	68,800	8,302	60,498
Talbot	22,800	1,866	20,934
Taliaferro	22,400	1,340	21,060
Tattnall	38,800	3,430	35,370
Taylor	31,600	1,978	29,622
Telfair	44,400	4,092	40,308
Terrell	47,600	3,679	43,921
Thomas	83,600	10,592	73,008
Tift	31,200	4,495	26,705
Toombs	37,200	3,842	33,358
Towns	10,400	626	9,774
Troy	91,600	11,337	80,263

TABLE X (Cont'd)

County	Cost of Minimum Program	Amount Raised by Uniform Local Tax	Amount Supplied by State
Treutlen	17,200	1,438	15,762
Turner	32,000	2,766	29,234
Twiggs	22,800	1,830	20,970
Union	14,400	760	13,640
Upson	46,800	3,898	42,902
Walker	56,400	6,429	49,971
Walton	63,600	4,008	59,592
Ware	72,000	9,207	62,793
Warren	33,600	1,924	31,676
Washington	60,000	5,774	54,226
Wayne	32,400	4,583	27,817
Webster	12,400	1,297	11,103
Wheeler	28,400	1,859	26,541
White	15,600	1,230	14,370
Whitfield	47,600	5,992	41,608
Wilcox	52,000	3,086	48,914
Wilkes	39,200	4,721	34,479
Wilkinson	27,200	8,201	18,999
Worth	69,200	4,441	64,759

The amount each county would raise by levying the uniform (.8 mills) local rate is shown in column two, Table X. Under the proposed plan, the state, in order to equalize the minimum offering, must supply the difference between the total cost of providing the offering as shown in column one, Table X, and the amount raised by levying the uniform local (.8 mills) tax upon the equalized valuation in that county, as shown in column two. This amount is shown in column three.

A single illustration will make clear the procedure employed in computing the amount the state must supply. The cost of providing the minimum educational offering in Appling County would be $32,000. The uniform local levy would produce $3,417. The uniform quota which the state must supply is the difference between $32,000 and $3,417, viz., $28,583.

It will be recalled that under our proposed plan, no county is to receive less from the state than the amount she now receives. Table XI shows the amount each county received from the state in 1925 in column two and in column one is shown the amount each county would receive under the proposed plan.

TABLE XI

COMPARISON OF STATE APPORTIONMENT FOR 1925
WITH APPORTIONMENT UNDER PROPOSED PLAN
(Based on $400 Per-Teacher Unit)

County	Amount Supplied by State Under Proposed Plan	State Apportionment for 1925
Appling	$28,583	$16,983
Atkinson	19,395	14,004
Bacon	19,960	10,181
Baker	19,473	11,730
Baldwin	38,758	22,182
Banks	32,852	15,473
Barrow	39,193	18,089
Bartow	53,370	35,044
Ben Hill	35,270	21,929
Berrien	46,384	20,282
Bibb	109,004	86,531
Bleckley	22,176	15,496
Brantley	17,365	9,391
Brooks	52,478	33,251
Bryan	18,493	9,253
Bulloch	67,751	42,056
Burke	49,844	39,729
Butts	23,661	16,588
Calhoun	20,297	14,439
Camden	16,324	9,395
Campbell	36,270	16,961
Candler	19,442	13,631
Carroll	80,832	48,400
Catoosa	15,138	10,501
Charlton	15,424	6,744
Chatham	120,230	102,990
Chattahoochee	7,134	5,568
Chattooga	29,382	20,517
Cherokee	45,558	28,776
Clarke	40,283	34,130
Clay	16,941	11,264
Clayton	27,424	14,821
Clinch	13,619	8,924
Cobb	76,068	41,776
Coffee	48,376	29,233
Colquitt	77,831	42,202
Columbia	25,037	15,589
Cook	35,958	17,356
Coweta	68,966	39,232
Crawford	18,349	15,074
Crisp	35,637	24,762
Dade	8,458	5,306
Dawson	8,682	5,772
Decatur	55,642	35,560

TABLE XI (Cont'd)

County	Amount Supplied by State Under Proposed Plan	State Apportionment for 1925
DeKalb	53,330	47,774
Dodge	45,319	37,398
Dooly	46,598	34,281
Dougherty	35,354	25,503
Douglas	22,996	14,341
Early	40,915	31,040
Echols	8,396	4,342
Effingham	27,708	16,916
Elbert	48,869	30,281
Emanuel	65,353	38,353
Evans	16,032	10,727
Fannin	28,876	17,569
Fayette	24,390	15,349
Floyd	83,982	53,409
Forsyth	30,079	15,860
Franklin	47,446	29,677
Fulton	499,198	292,041
Gilmer	23,387	13,560
Glascock	12,485	6,260
Glynn	22,050	22,529
Gordon	47,233	23,563
Grady	54,948	30,352
Greene	34,406	24,749
Gwinnett	78,032	41,612
Habersham	27,190	19,012
Hall	59,151	39,267
Hancock	34,442	24,207
Haralson	48,512	20,766
Harris	30,402	21,911
Hart	45,321	27,017
Heard	41,628	15,971
Henry	43,000	25,641
Houston	43,674	33,060
Irwin	33,117	19,842
Jackson	55,842	32,967
Jasper	33,118	19,727
Jeff Davis	26,158	12,046
Jefferson	42,257	31,710
Jenkins	23,152	18,857
Johnson	37,689	19,647
Jones	31,795	17,769
Lamar	19,458	15,527
Lanier	12,732	7,122
Laurens	90,903	52,778
Lee	29,242	15,256
Liberty	24,174	12,783
Lincoln	26,307	13,946
Long	9,258	5,954
Lowndes	60,049	36,195

TABLE XI (Cont'd)

County	Amount Supplied by State Under Proposed Plan	State Apportionment for 1925
Lumpkin	10,476	7,344
Macon	36,851	23,483
Madison	44,446	24,811
Marion	19,201	11,238
Meriwether	48,110	34,055
Miller	21,905	13,808
Milton	17,702	9,479
Mitchell	53,122	39,449
Monroe	29,038	21,219
Montgomery	23,473	16,317
Morgan	35,155	22,826
Murray	21,967	13,045
Muscogee	88,206	62,000
McDuffie	24,263	14,399
McIntosh	14,697	8,862
Newton	50,932	32,771
Oconee	24,320	12,254
Oglethorpe	40,342	23,954
Paulding	35,911	18,723
Pickens	24,790	12,738
Pierce	28,662	16,614
Pike	27,989	18,941
Polk	55,698	30,942
Pulaski	21,238	15,420
Putnam	23,454	20,131
Quitman	6,424	5,586
Rabun	12,749	8,840
Randolph	33,642	27,284
Richmond	83,187	83,756
Rockdale	22,142	12,050
Schley	18,631	8,765
Screven	46,620	33,566
Seminole	20,838	12,530
Spaulding	43,109	31,884
Stephens	30,071	17,920
Stewart	28,350	18,448
Sumter	60,498	39,307
Talbot	20,934	14,918
Taliaferro	21,060	11,104
Tattnall	35,370	23,874
Taylor	29,622	18,830
Telfair	40,308	26,374
Terrell	43,921	30,072
Thomas	73,008	41,012
Tift	26,705	21,720
Toombs	33,358	20,983
Towns	9,774	5,772
Troup	80,263	52,166
Treutlen	15,762	11,566

TABLE XI (Cont'd)

County	Amount Supplied by State Under Proposed Plan	State Apportionment for 1925
Turner	29,234	18,164
Twiggs	20,970	16,188
Union	13,640	9,555
Upson	42,902	27,834
Walker	49,971	33,233
Walton	59,592	28,678
Ware	62,793	32,998
Warren	31,676	16,996
Washington	54,226	37,913
Wayne	27,817	17,085
Webster	11,103	7,819
Wheeler	26,541	14,870
White	14,370	10,012
Whitfield	41,608	28,887
Wilcox	48,914	22,600
Wilkes	34,479	27,026
Wilkinson	18,999	19,163
Worth	64,759	31,999

A careful study of Table XI will reveal three things: (1) that no county will receive less from the state under the proposed plan than she now receives; (2) that all but one county will receive more than she now receives; and (3) that the percentage of increase in the amount each county receives from the state becomes larger as the ability of the county decreases. By this means, the poorer counties will receive proportionately more from the state and will be able to provide at least the minimum offering.

Thus far the present chapter has pointed out the evils resulting from present methods of distributing state aid. Three outstanding systems of school support, the advantages and disadvantages of each, were also considered. Following these considerations, a plan of support applicable to the state of Georgia was presented and definitely applied.

The cost to the state of providing the minimum offering (represented by an expenditure of $400 per teacher unit) called for by this plan was found to be $6,305,399. Table XI shows that the amount provided from state funds and distributed to the counties in 1925 was approximately $4,000,000. It is evident that in order to put the proposed plan into operation, the state must provide additional funds to the amount of $2,305,399. The necessity for these additional funds and the obligation of the state to provide them have been pointed out and, consequently, need not be dwelt upon further. The necessity for additional revenue at once raises the question as to the sources from which such revenues shall be derived.

Although it does not lie within the scope of the present account to enter upon a detailed study either of existing or of potential sources of school revenue in Georgia, it nevertheless seems advisable to give at least brief consideration to certain aspects of the problem. The tendency to utilize the state personal income tax as a source of revenue was well under way when in 1914 it was given a distinct setback by the provision for a federal income tax. With the reduction of the rates of the federal income tax, this tendency will in all probability receive new impetus. Massachusetts, Delaware, and North Carolina at the present time derive the major portion of school revenues furnished by the state from the proceeds of state personal income taxes. Georgia would do well to follow the example of these three states. Another source of revenue would be some form of luxury tax.[10]

Chapter IV called attention to the fact that property in Georgia is equalized at only 35 per cent of its true value, and recommended assessment on the basis of true value. This reform is urged not only on the basis of the soundness and equity of such procedure, but because it is believed that such a policy will result in increased revenues. Without the provision of new sources of revenue or general and fundamental reforms in taxation, the only possibility of providing the additional revenues required for the proposed program obviously lies in an increased state millage, or in reducing the amounts of revenue not appropriated for other public projects and diverting to the schools the sums thus made available. From this consideration of the additional revenues required and policies of taxation affecting the same, we now turn to the concluding chapter of the present study, which will attempt to bring together in brief summary form the program and recommendations thus far presented.

[10] For a fuller consideration of potential sources of school revenue, see F. H. Swift, *State Policies in Public School Finance.*

CHAPTER VI

SUMMARY AND CONCLUSIONS

In the opening chapter of the present study, it was stated that the solution would be presented in the following four divisions: (1) the measurement of educational need; (2) the determination of the minimum offering to be equalized and supported by the state; (3) an adequate measurement of the financial ability of local school units,—the counties; (4) a plan of school support.

Each of these divisions of the problem has been treated, successively, in preceding chapters. It is the purpose of this, the final chapter, to summarize the most important conclusions arrived at in earlier chapters, together with certain other recommendations implied in the principles which have been set forth or which grow out of practical considerations in the Georgia school situation. Without further introduction, attention will be directed to the recommendations themselves, which, for the sake of convenience, will be presented in numbered paragraphs.

1. The minimum educational offering which the state of Georgia shall undertake to equalize at the present time shall be that represented in an expenditure of $400 per teacher unit. It should be borne in mind that this $400 offering represents an offering far below the average provided within the state at the present time, and has been suggested for reasons of expediency merely as the first step of a progressive program, the goal of which is to equalize within a comparatively short time the state average offering, whatever that may be, now found to be $700 per teacher unit.

2. In measuring educational need, one teacher and only one shall be allowed for every one-teacher school.

3. In measuring the educational need of all the schools employing two or more teachers, the teacher allowance shall be one teacher for every 30 pupils in average daily attendance and a proportionate teacher allowance for every additional 30 pupils in average daily attendance, or fraction thereof.

4. As a prerequisite to participating in state funds, counties shall be required to report all data necessary for putting into effect the proposed program. Conspicuous among the reforms which must be inaugurated are the following:

    a Reporting average daily attendance by schools.

    b A distinction between capital outlay and current expenses.

    c The separation of all data reported for white schools from all data reported for colored schools.

5. All moneys provided for the minimum offering shall be used for current expenses only, and 80 per cent of all such moneys furnished by the state and 80 per cent of all such moneys furnished by the counties shall be devoted to paying teachers salaries.

6. In order that the plan of school support presented in Chapter V may be put into effect with facility, the present method of distributing the state school fund shall be abandoned.

7. The state department of education shall set up a uniform system of school accounting and budgetary procedure to be adopted by all local units. The forms necessary for putting this system into effect, together with a handbook of instructions, shall be supplied at the expense of the state to all local school units.

8. A more scientific method of assessment should be employed, and real or true values shall be made the basis of taxation.

9. A more adequate and equitable system of taxation shall be inaugurated, which will tap all sources of revenue and provide that the burden of taxation be distributed equally in proportion to ability to pay, and thus make it possible for every community to provide as good schools as it may desire.

BIBLIOGRAPHY

UNITED STATES DOCUMENTS AND REPORTS

Bureau of Census, Department of Commerce. *Financial Statistics of Cities, 1922 State Compendium for Georgia.*

Bureau of Education, Department of Interior. *Educational Study of Alabama.* United States Bureau of Education Bulletin, 1919, No. 41.

Bureau of Internal Revenue, Department of Treasury. *Statistics of Income, 1922.*

BOOKS

Alexander, Carter. *Bibliography on Educational Finance.* New York: The Macmillan Co., 1924

Brooks, R. P. *History of Georgia.* New York: Atkinson, Mentzer and Company

Cubberley, Ellwood P. *School Funds and Their Apportionment.* New York: Teachers College, Bureau of Publications, 1906

Cubberly, Ellwood P. *State and County Educational Reorganization; The Revised Constitution and School Code of the State of Osceola.* New York: The Macmillan Company, 1914

Cubberley, Ellwood P. and Sears, Jesse B. *The Cost of Education in California.* New York: The Macmillan Company, 1924

Evenden, Edward S. *Teachers Salaries and Salary Trends in 1923.* Washington: National Education Association, 1923

Keith, John A. H. and Bagley, William C. *The Nation and the Schools.* New York: Macmillan Company, 1920

New York State. *Joint Committee on Rural Schools.* Rural School Survey of New York State. Vol. I, Preliminary Report. Ithaca, 1922

McGaughy, J. R. *The Fiscal Administration of City School Systems.* New York: The Macmillan Company, 1924

Morrison, Henry C. *Financing of Public Schools in the State of Illinois.* New York: The Macmillan Company, 1924

Mort, Paul R. *The Measurement of Educational Need.* New York: Teachers College, Bureau of Publications, 1924

Mort, Paul R., and others. *A Report on State Aid for the Public Schools in the State of New York.* Albany: J. B. Lyon, 1925

Newcomer, Mabel. *Financial Statistics of Public Education in the United States, 1910-20.* New York: The Macmillan Company, 1924

Reeves, Floyd W. *The Political Unit of Public School Finance in Illinois.* New York: The Macmillan Company, 1924

Russell, Wm. F., Holy, T. C. and Stone, R. W. *Financing of Education in Iowa.* New York: The Macmillan Company, 1925

Seligman, E. R. A. *Essays in Taxation.* New York: The Macmillan Company, 1923. Ninth Edition.

Seligman, E. R. A. *Essays in Taxation.* London: The Macmillan Company, 1913

Strayer, George D. and Haig, Robert M. *The Financing of Education in the State of New York.* New York: The Macmillan Company, 1923

Strayer, George D. and others. *Report of the Survey of Certain Aspects of the Public School System of Springfield, Massachusetts, for the School Year, 1923-24.* New York: Teachers College, Institute of Educational Research, Division of Field Studies, 1924

Strayer, George D. and others. *Report of the Survey of Certain Aspects of the Public School System of Providence, Rhode Island, for the School Year 1923-24.* Providence: The Oxford Press, 1924

Stoops, R. O. *Elementary School Costs in the State of New York.* New York: The Macmillan Company, 1924 .

Swift, Fletcher H. *Studies in Public School Finance. The West.* Minneapolis: University of Minnesota, Research Publications, Education Series, 1922. No. 1.

Swift, Fletcher Harper. *Studies in Public School Finance. The East.* Minneapolis: University of Minnesota, Research Publications, Education Series, 1923. No. 2.

Swift, Fletcher Harper. *Public Permanent Common School Funds in the United States*. New York: Henry Holt and Company, 1911

ARTICLES

Alexander, Carter. Comparative State School Aids. *Elementary School Journal* 21: 522-28. March, 1921

Alexander, Carter. Larger State Distributive School Fund for Illinois. *School and Society* 12: 565-76. December 11, 1920

Alexander, Carter. Opportunities for Research in Educational Finance. *Educational Administrative and Supervision,* 9: 209-22, April, 1923

Folks, Gertrude. State Funds for Public Schools. *Elementary School Journal,* 20:269-80. January, 1920

McGaughy, J. R. The Superintendent's Analysis of School Finance. *Teachers College Record,* 26:383-92, 660-70, January and April, 1925

New York's Rural Schools. (Editorial)*Educational Review,* 65: 338-42. November 1922

Swift, Fletcher Harper. Common School Finance in Alabama. *Educational Administration and Supervision,* 5: 303-24. September, 1919; 365-86, October, 1919.

Smith, Payson A. Program for Education in Massachusetts. Harvard's Teacher's Association. *School and Society,* 10: 715-20, December 20, 1919

Strayer, George D. Support of Public Education. *Journal of Educational Research,* 5:331-32, April, 1922

Strayer, George D. Financing Public Education. *Teachers College Record.* XXVI: 145-50. October, 1924

GEORGIA

Department of Education
  Georgia State School Items, Vol. I, No. 1-21, 1924
  Annual Reports, 1922, 1923
  Census of School Population of Georgia, 1923
  School Code, 1923
  Georgia State School Items, Vol. II, 1925
State Tax Commissioner
  Annual Reports, 1919-23

GENERAL

Public Education in Kentucky. Report. General Education Board, 1922. 190-202

National Education Association. *Teachers' Salaries and Salary Trends.* Washington: National Education Association, 1923

MAGAZINES

Journal of Educational Research. Bloomington, Illinois. Educational Research Association

Teachers College Record. New York: Teachers College, Bureau of Publications